1 Sea Otter

■ Draw a line from the arrow (➡) to the star (★) by following the path.

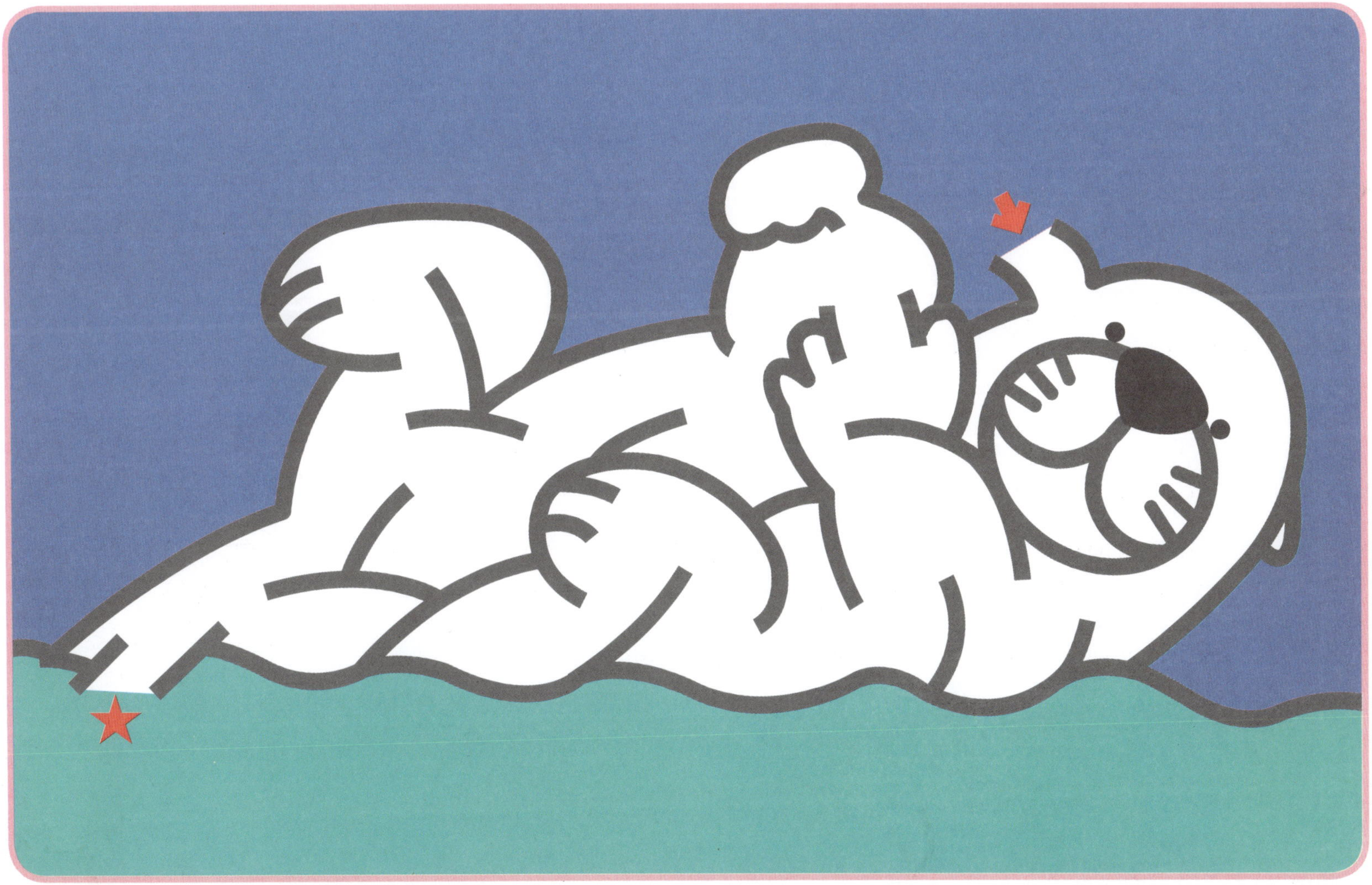

■ Draw a line from the arrow (➡) to the star (★) by following the path.

2 Seal

Name

Date

■ Draw a line from the arrow (➡) to the star (★) by following the path.

■ Draw a line from the arrow (➡) to the star (★) by following the path.

3 Tapir

Name

Date

■ Draw a line from the arrow (➡) to the star (★) by following the path.

5

■ Draw a line from the arrow (→) to the star (★) by following the path.

4 Bat

Name

Date

■ Draw a line from the arrow (➡) to the star (★) by following the path.

■ Draw a line from the arrow (➜) to the star (★) by following the path.

5 Kangaroo and Kid

Name

Date

■ Draw a line from the arrow (➡) to the star (★) by following the path.

■ Draw a line from the arrow (➡) to the star (★) by following the path.

Mandrill

Name

Date

■ Draw a line from the arrow (→) to the star (★) by following the path.

11

■ Draw a line from the arrow (➡) to the star (★) by following the path.

Reindeer

Name

Date

■ Draw a line from the arrow (→) to the star (★) by following the path.

■ Draw a line from the arrow (➡) to the star (★) by following the path.

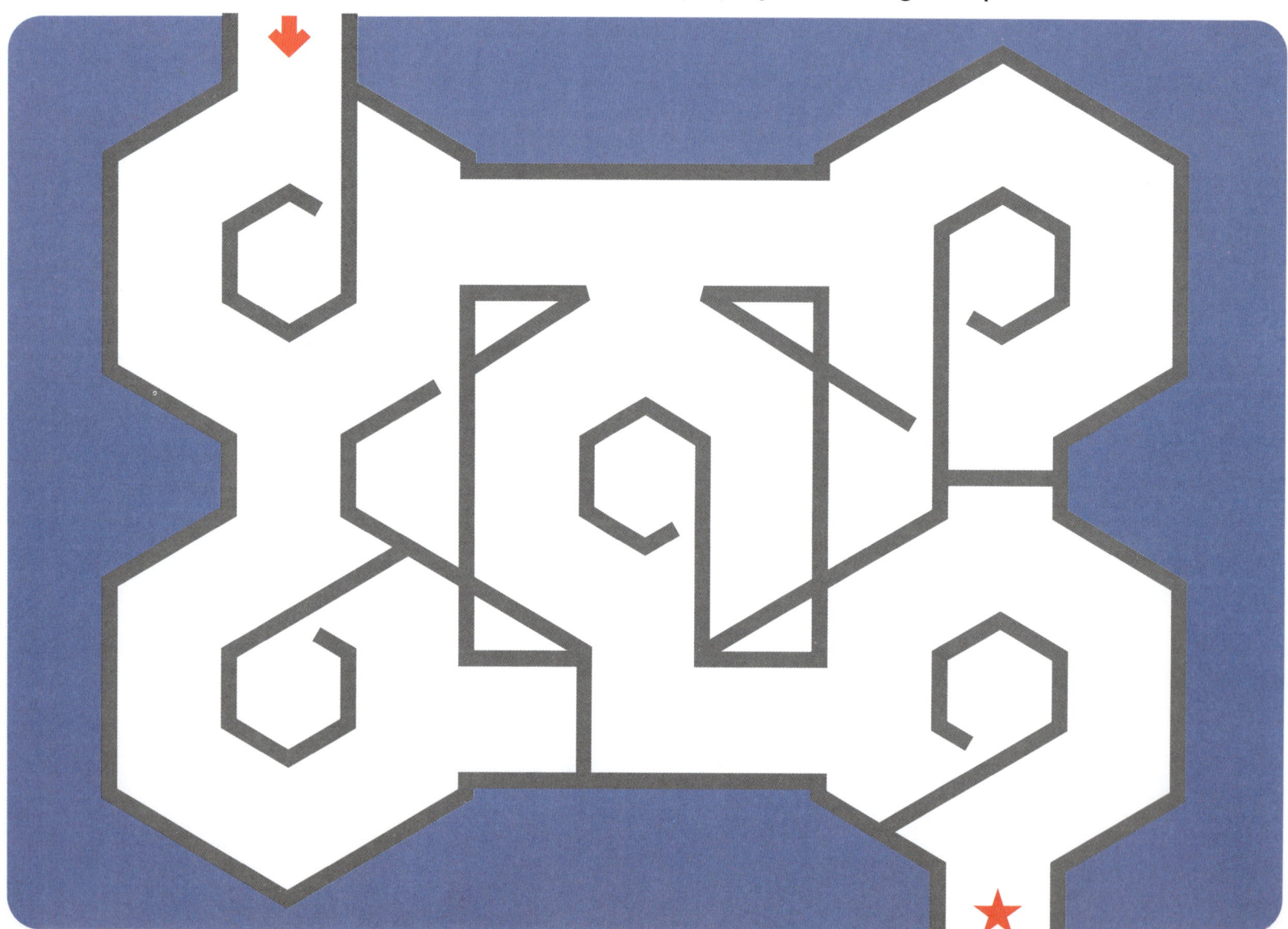

8 Bee

Name

Date

■ Draw a line from the arrow (→) to the star (★) by following the path.

15

■ Draw a line from the arrow (→) to the star (★) by following the path.

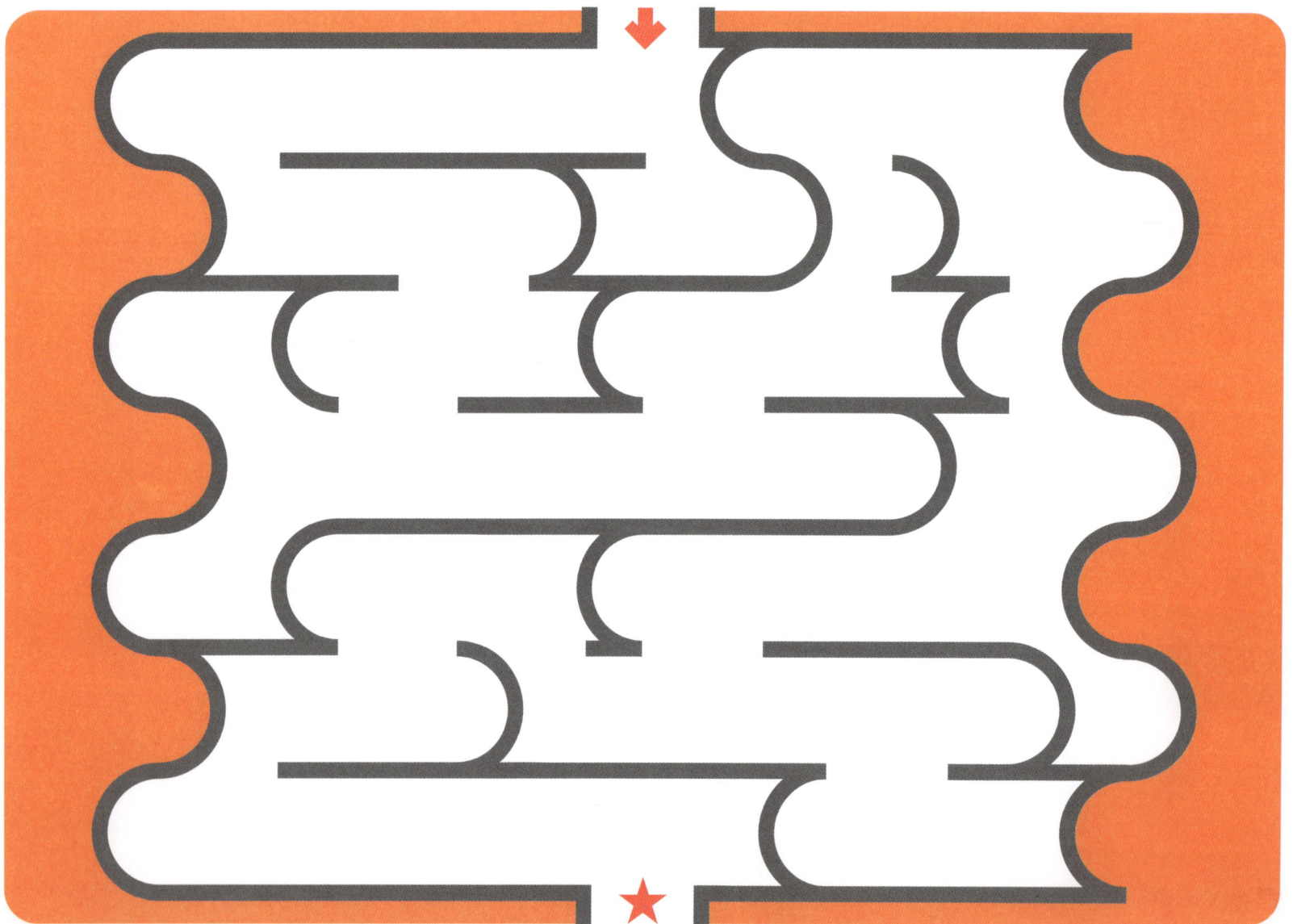

Songbird

Name

Date

■ Draw a line from the arrow (➜) to the star (★) by following the path.

■ Draw a line from the arrow (→) to the star (★) by following the path.

10 Mantis

Name

Date

■ Draw a line from the arrow (➡) to the star (★) by following the path.

■ Draw a line from the arrow (→) to the star (★) by following the path.

Rooster

Name

Date

■ Draw a line from the arrow (→) to the star (★) by following the path.

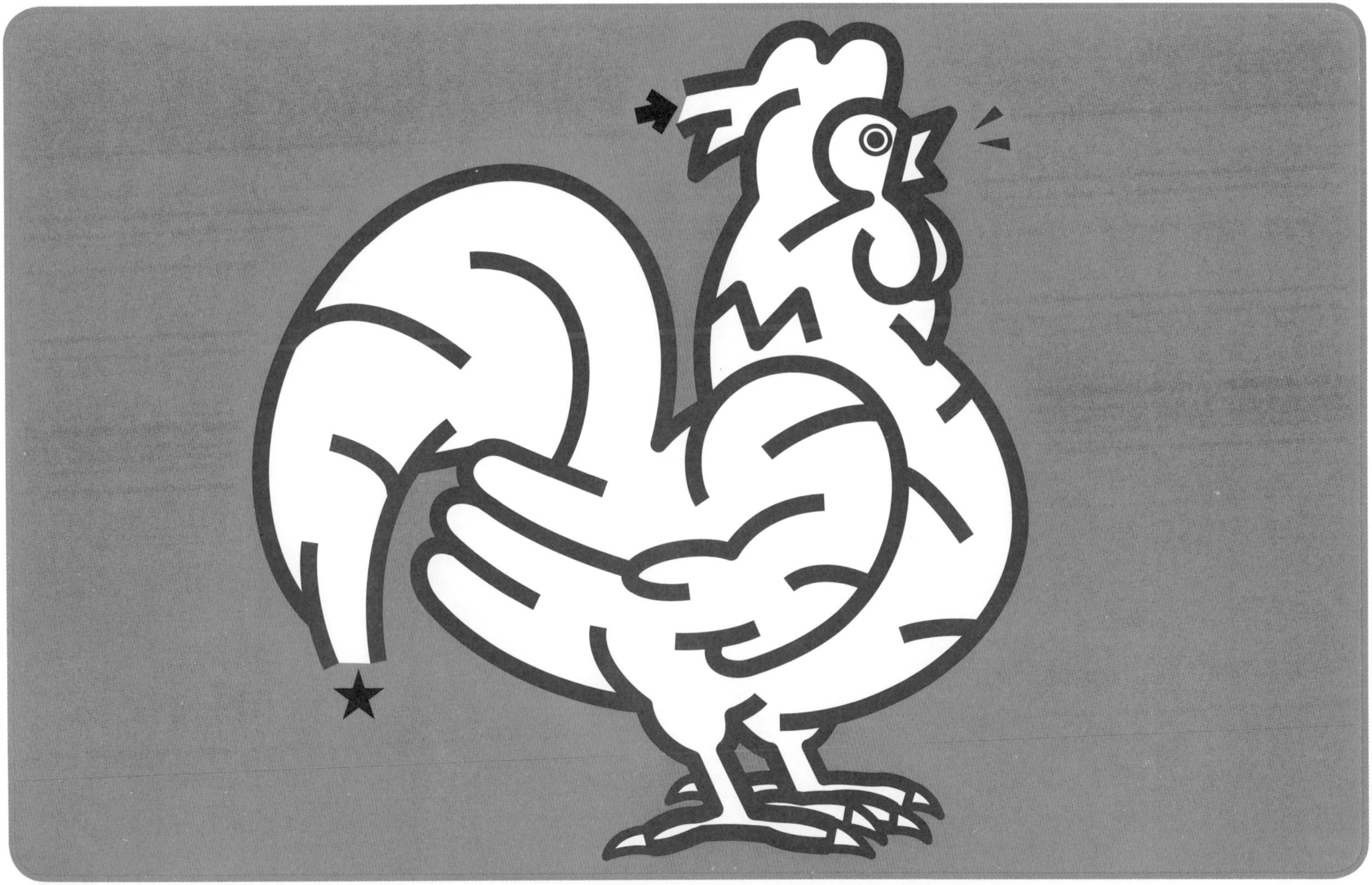

■ Draw a line from the arrow (➡) to the star (★) by following the path.

12 Pelican

Name

Date

■ Draw a line from the arrow (➡) to the star (★) by following the path.

23

■ Draw a line from the arrow (➡) to the star (★) by following the path.

13 Squid

Name

Date

■ Draw a line from the arrow (➡) to the star (★) by following the path.

■ Draw a line from the arrow (➡) to the star (★) by following the path.

14 Hermit Crab

Name

Date

■ Draw a line from the arrow (➡) to the star (★) by following the path.

27

■ Draw a line from the arrow (➡) to the star (★) by following the path.

15 Bag

■ Draw a line from the arrow (➜) to the star (★) by following the path.

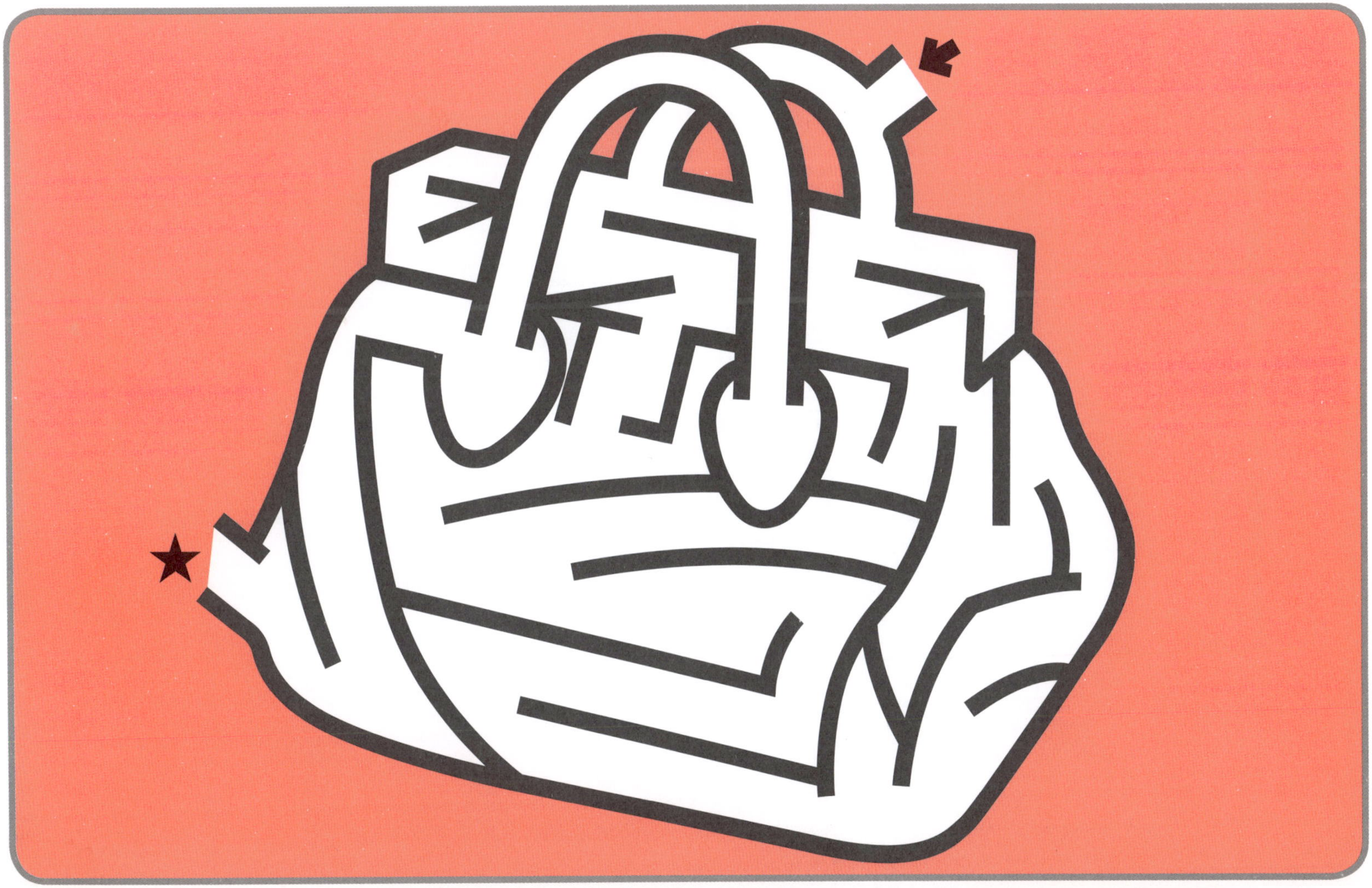

■ Draw a line from the arrow (➡) to the star (★) by following the path.

16 Watering Can

Name

Date

■ Draw a line from the arrow (➜) to the star (★) by following the path.

31

■ Draw a line from the arrow (➡) to the star (★) by following the path.

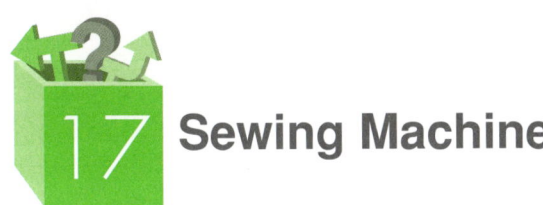

Sewing Machine

- Draw a line from the arrow (➡) to the star (★) by following the path.

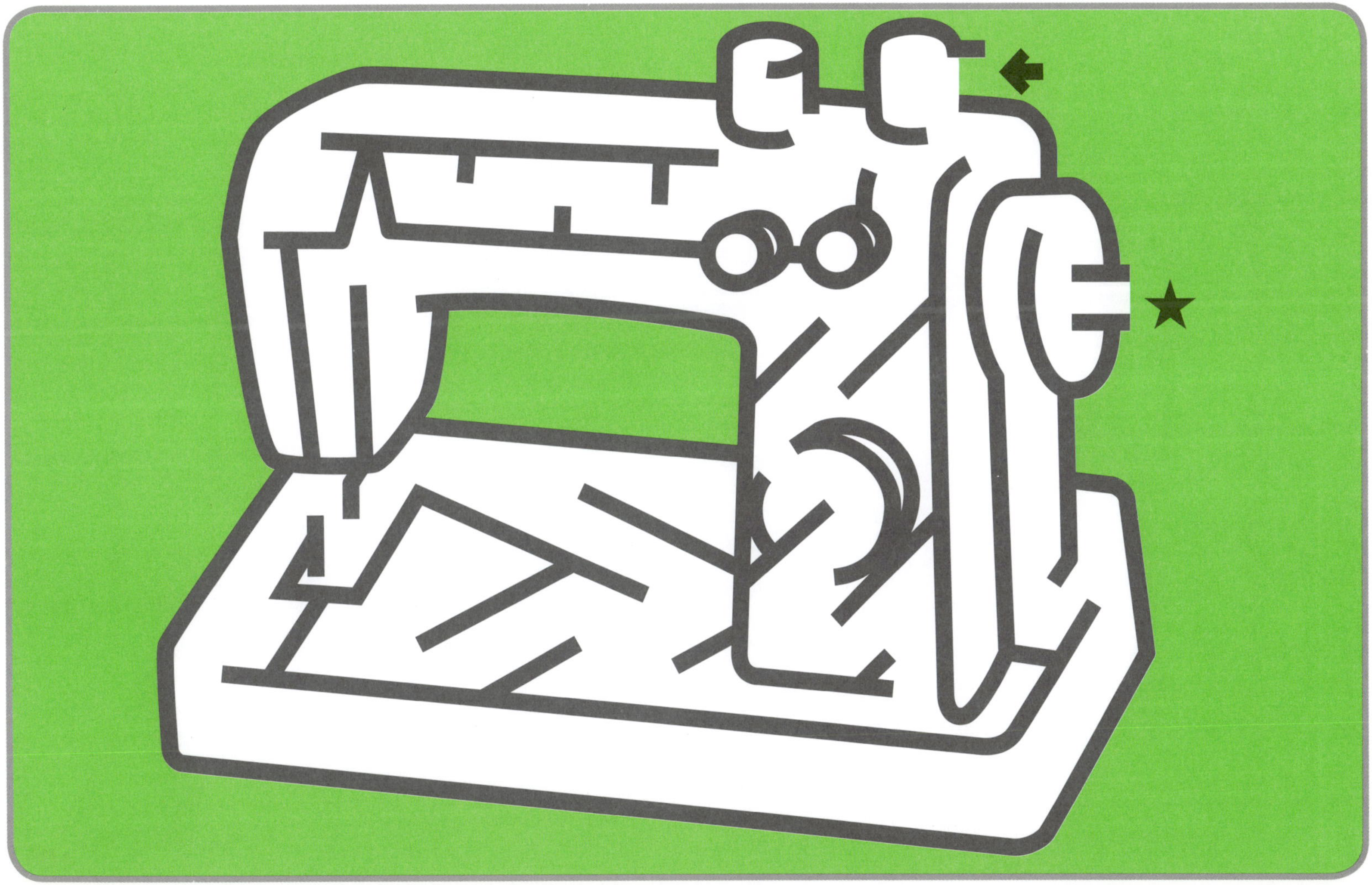

■ Draw a line from the arrow (→) to the star (★) by following the path.

18 Fishing Panda

Name

Date

■ Draw a line from the arrow (➡) to the star (★) by following the path.

■ Draw a line from the arrow (➡) to the star (★) by following the path.

19

Bow Wow Blues

Name

Date

■ Draw a line from the arrow (➔) to the star (★) by following the path.

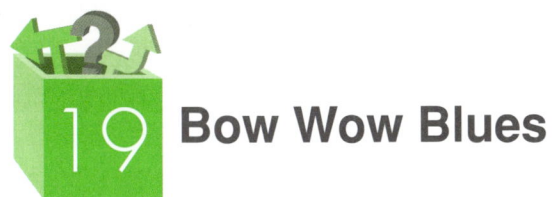

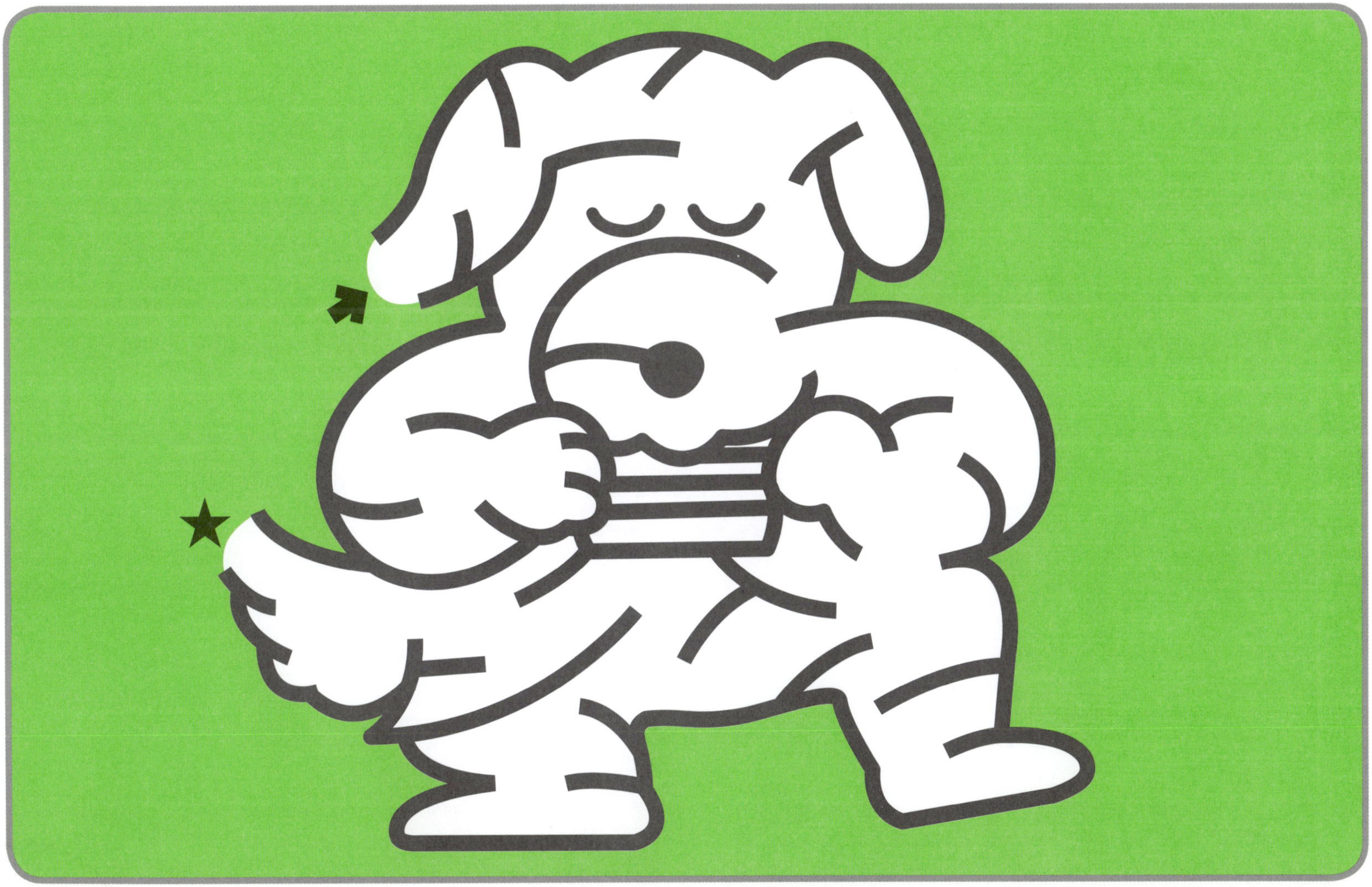

■ Draw a line from the arrow (➡) to the star (★) by following the path.

20 Monkeying Around

Name

Date

■ Draw a line from the arrow (➔) to the star (★) by following the path.

■ Draw a line from the arrow (➡) to the star (★) by following the path.

Trumpeting Pig

■ Draw a line from the arrow (➜) to the star (★) by following the path.

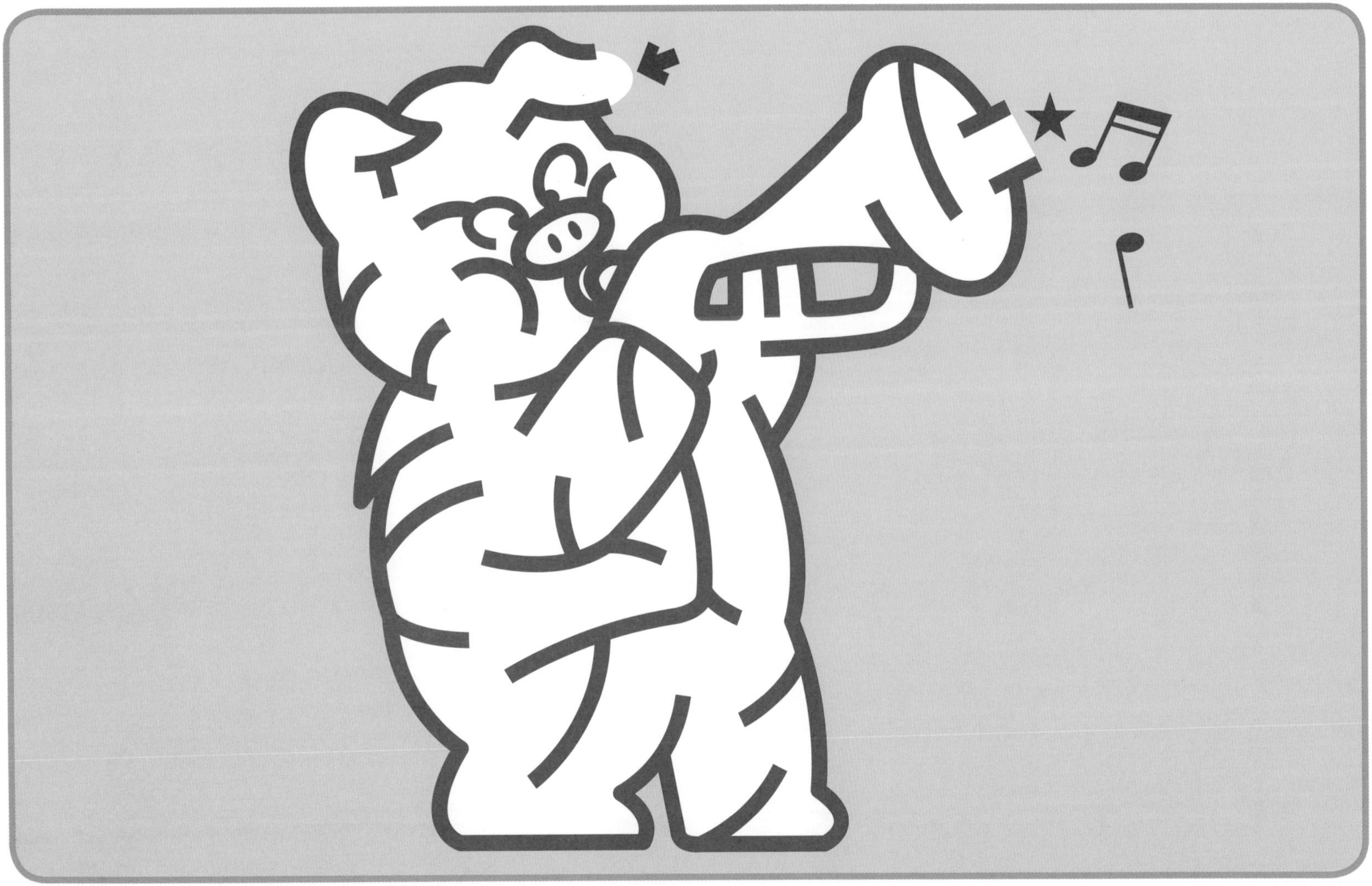

■ Draw a line from the arrow (➡) to the star (★) by following the path.

22 Dog Archer

Name

Date

■ Draw a line from the arrow (➔) to the star (★) by following the path.

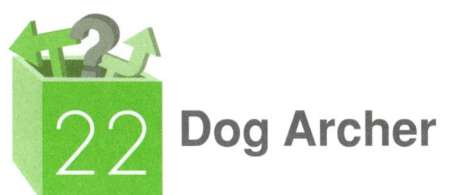

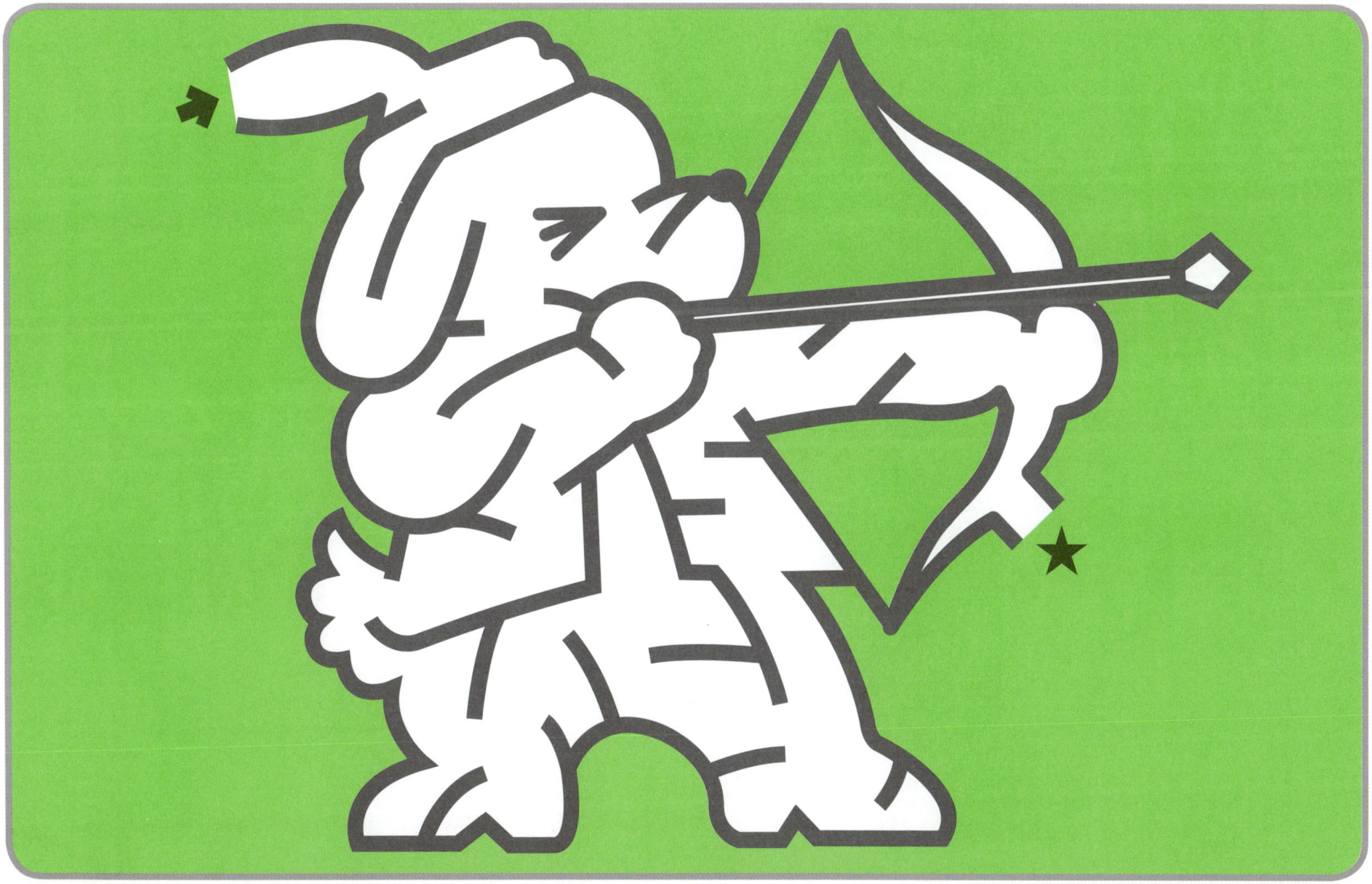

■ Draw a line from the arrow (→) to the star (★) by following the path.

Cat Concert

■ Draw a line from the arrow (➜) to the star (★) by following the path.

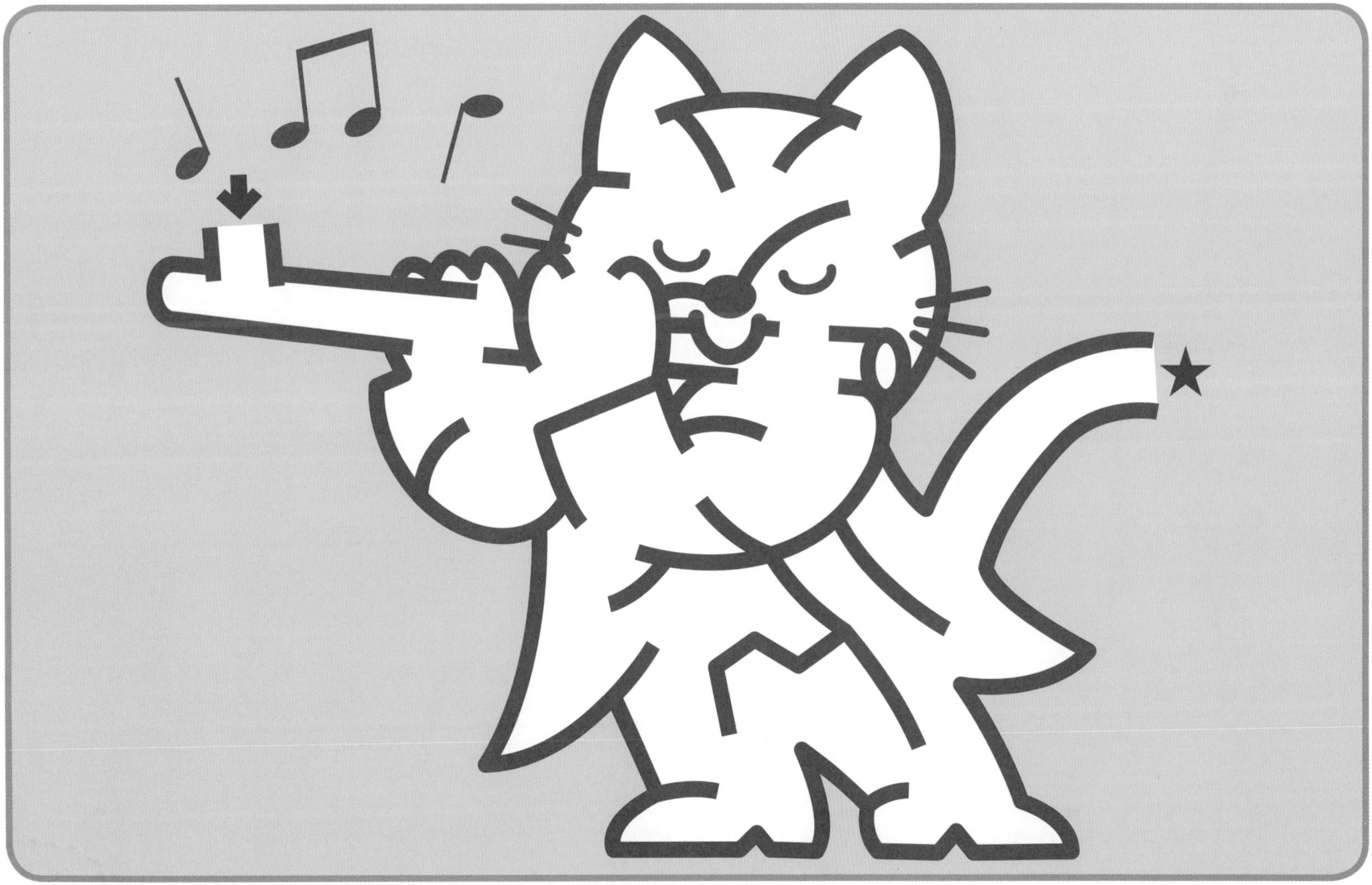

■ Draw a line from the arrow (➡) to the star (★) by following the path.

24 Ostrich Rock and Roll

Name

Date

■ Draw a line from the arrow (➡) to the star (★) by following the path.

47

■ Draw a line from the arrow (➡) to the star (★) by following the path.

25 Bear Beats

Name	
Date	

■ Draw a line from the arrow (➔) to the star (★) by following the path.

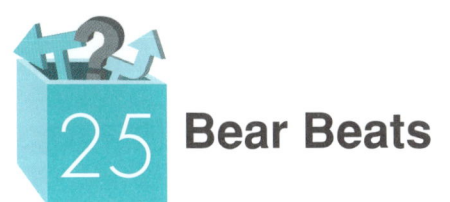

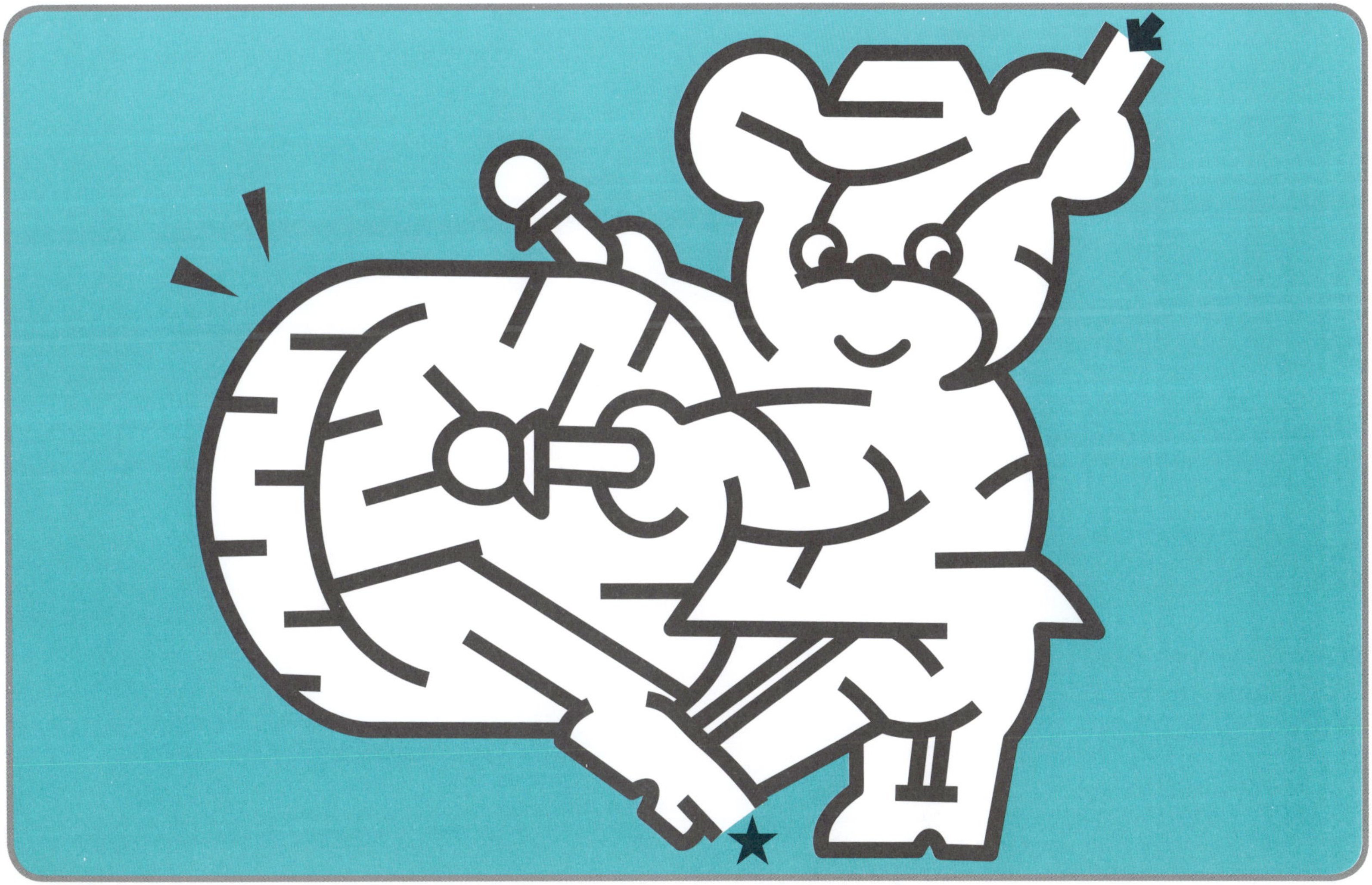

■ Draw a line from the arrow (➡) to the star (★) by following the path.

26 Humpback Whale

Name

Date

■ Draw a line from the arrow (➡) to the star (★) by following the path.

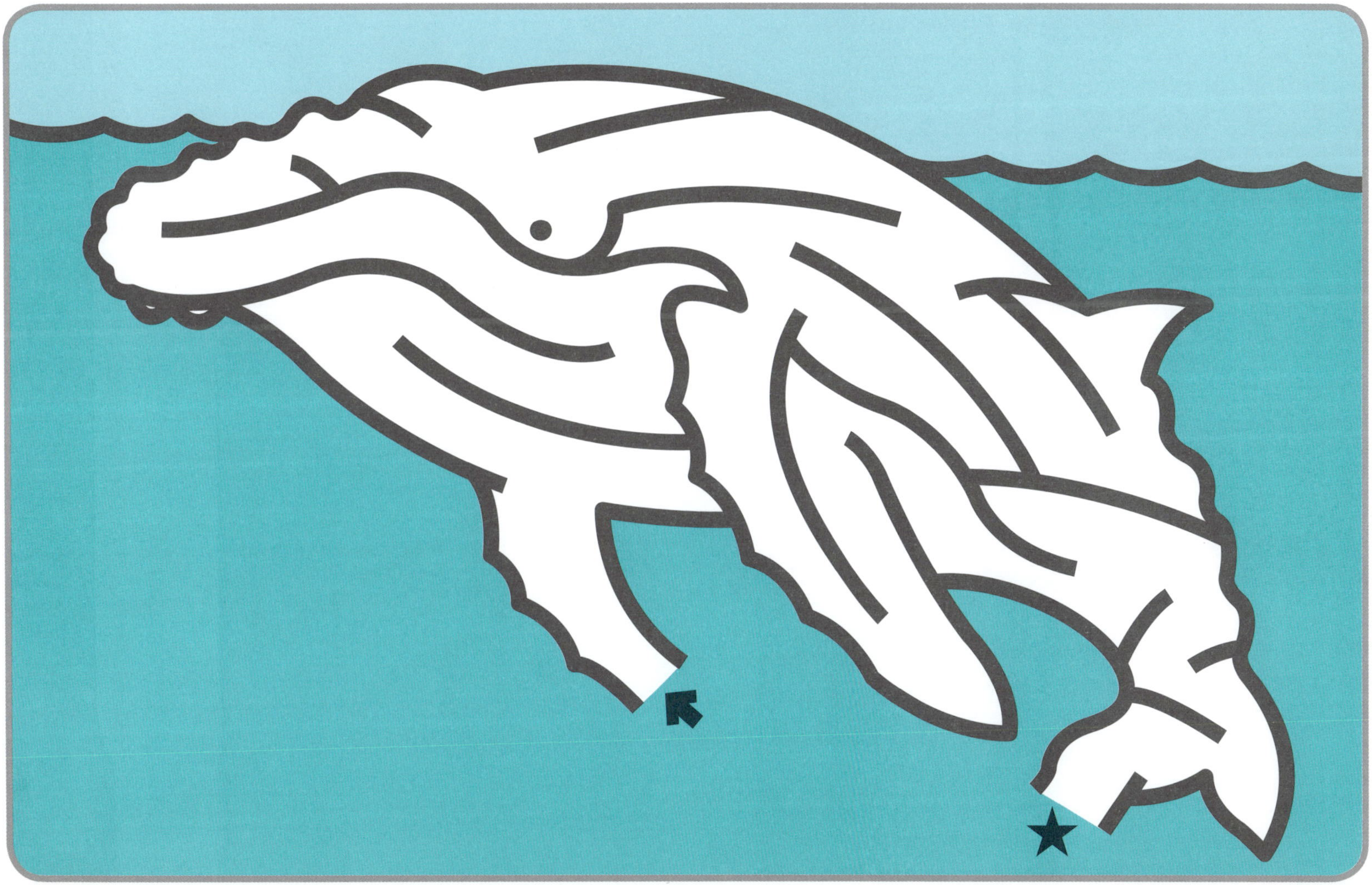

51

■ Draw a line from the arrow (➡) to the star (★) by following the path.

27 Fin Whale

■ Draw a line from the arrow (➡) to the star (★) by following the path.

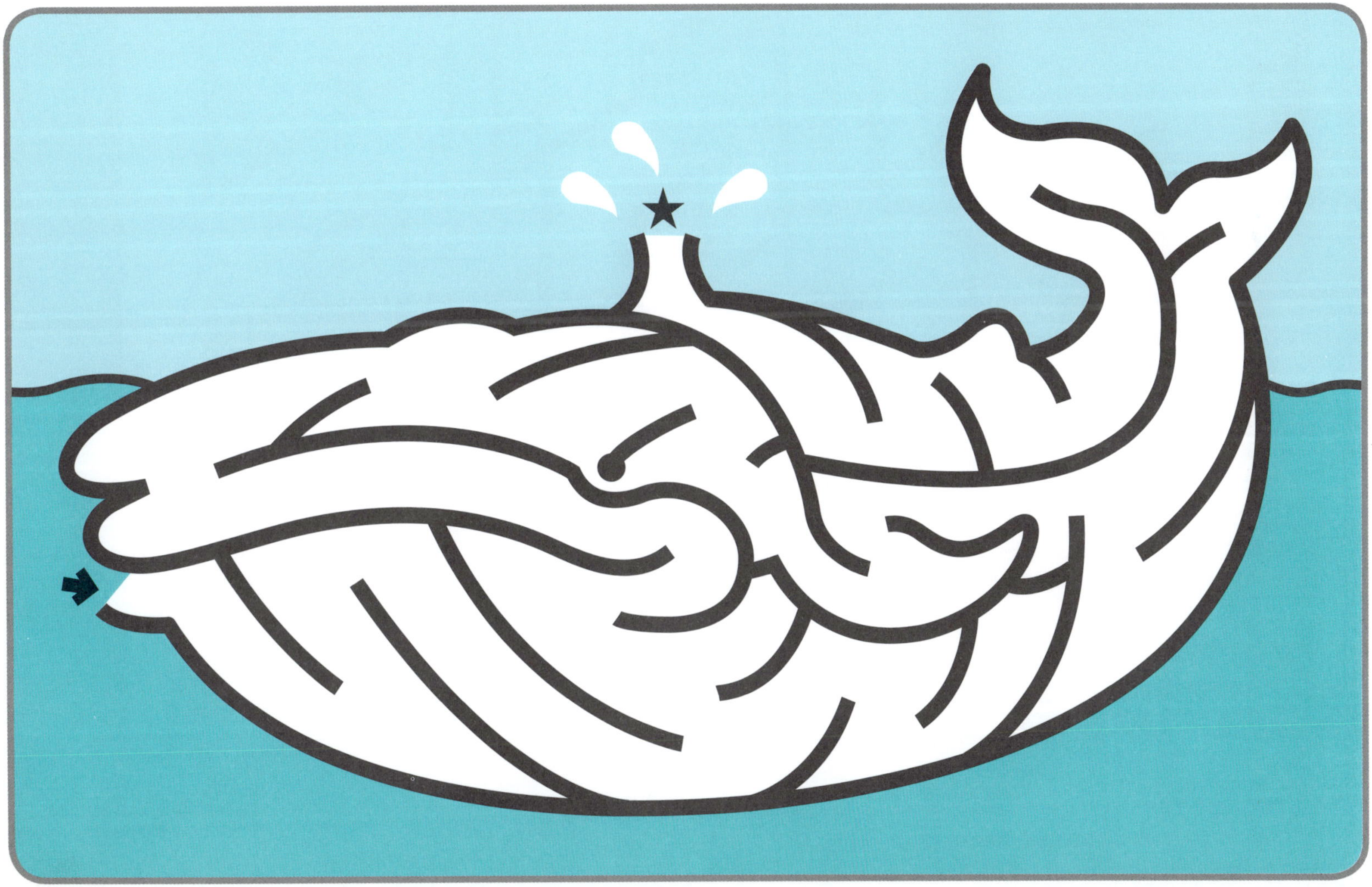

53

■ Draw a line from the arrow (➡) to the star (★) by following the path.

28 Right Whale

■ Draw a line from the arrow (➡) to the star (★) by following the path.

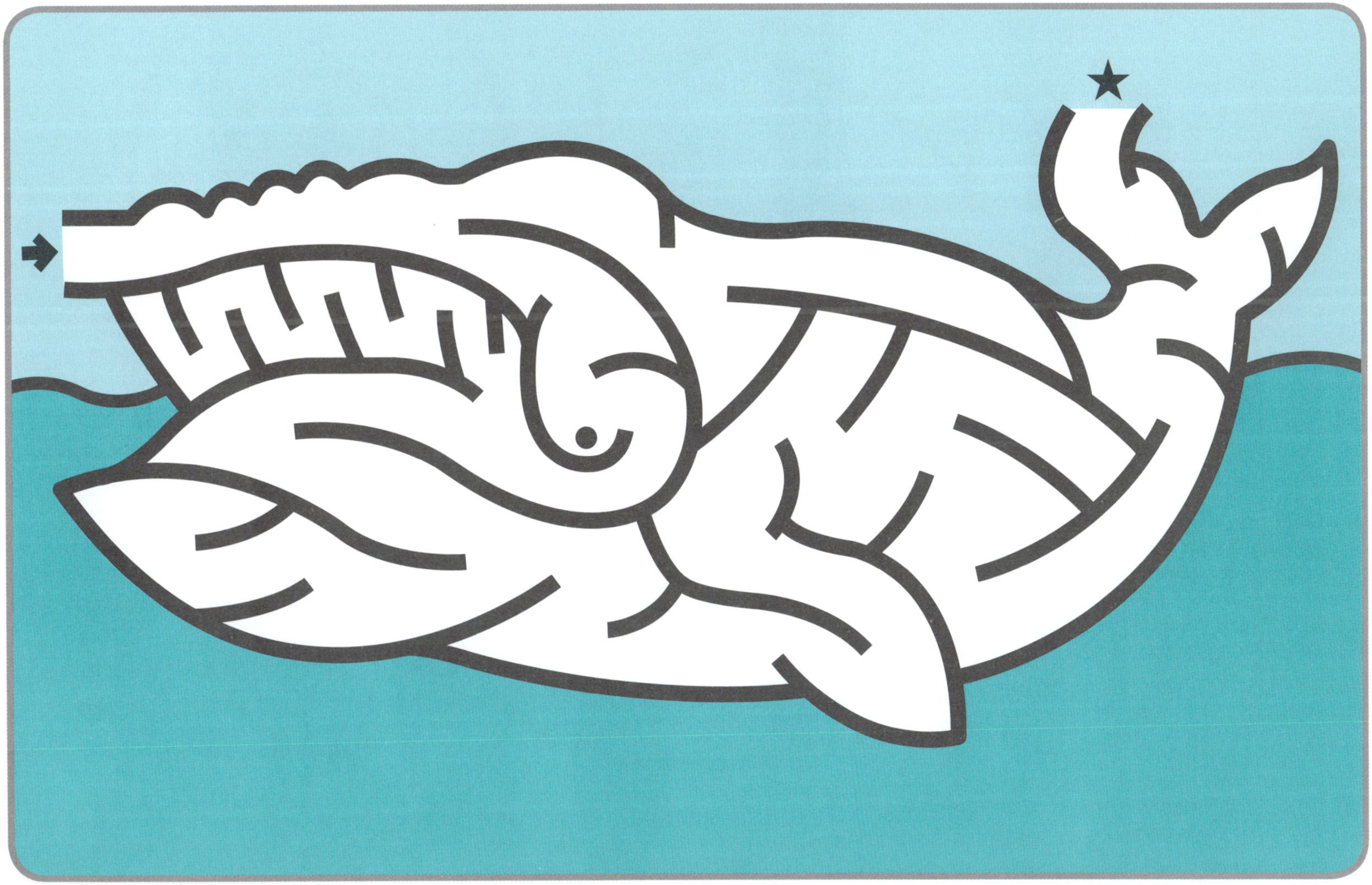

■ Draw a line from the arrow (→) to the star (★) by following the path.

29. Sperm Whale

Name

Date

■ Draw a line from the arrow (➔) to the star (★) by following the path.

57

■ Draw a line from the arrow (➡) to the star (★) by following the path.

30 Tyrannosaurus

Name

Date

■ Draw a line from the arrow (➔) to the star (★) by following the path.

■ Draw a line from the arrow (→) to the star (★) by following the path.

31 Stegosaurus

■ Draw a line from the arrow (➡) to the star (★) by following the path.

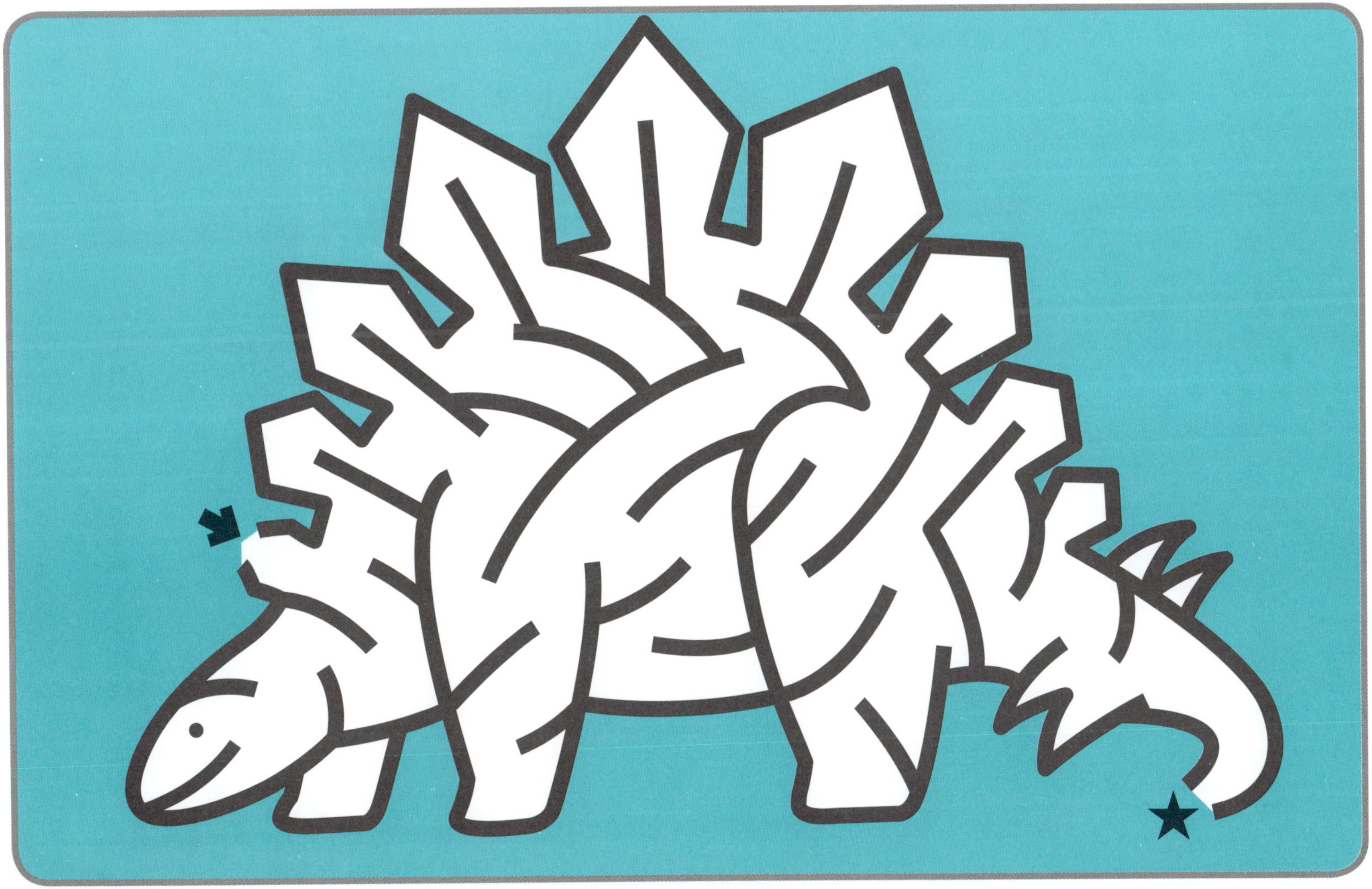

■ Draw a line from the arrow (→) to the star (★) by following the path.

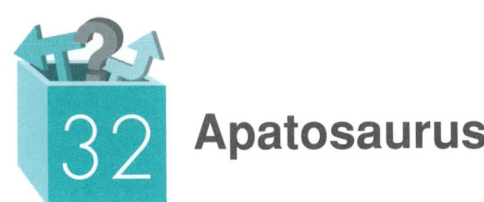

32 Apatosaurus

Name
Date

- Draw a line from the arrow (➔) to the star (★) by following the path.

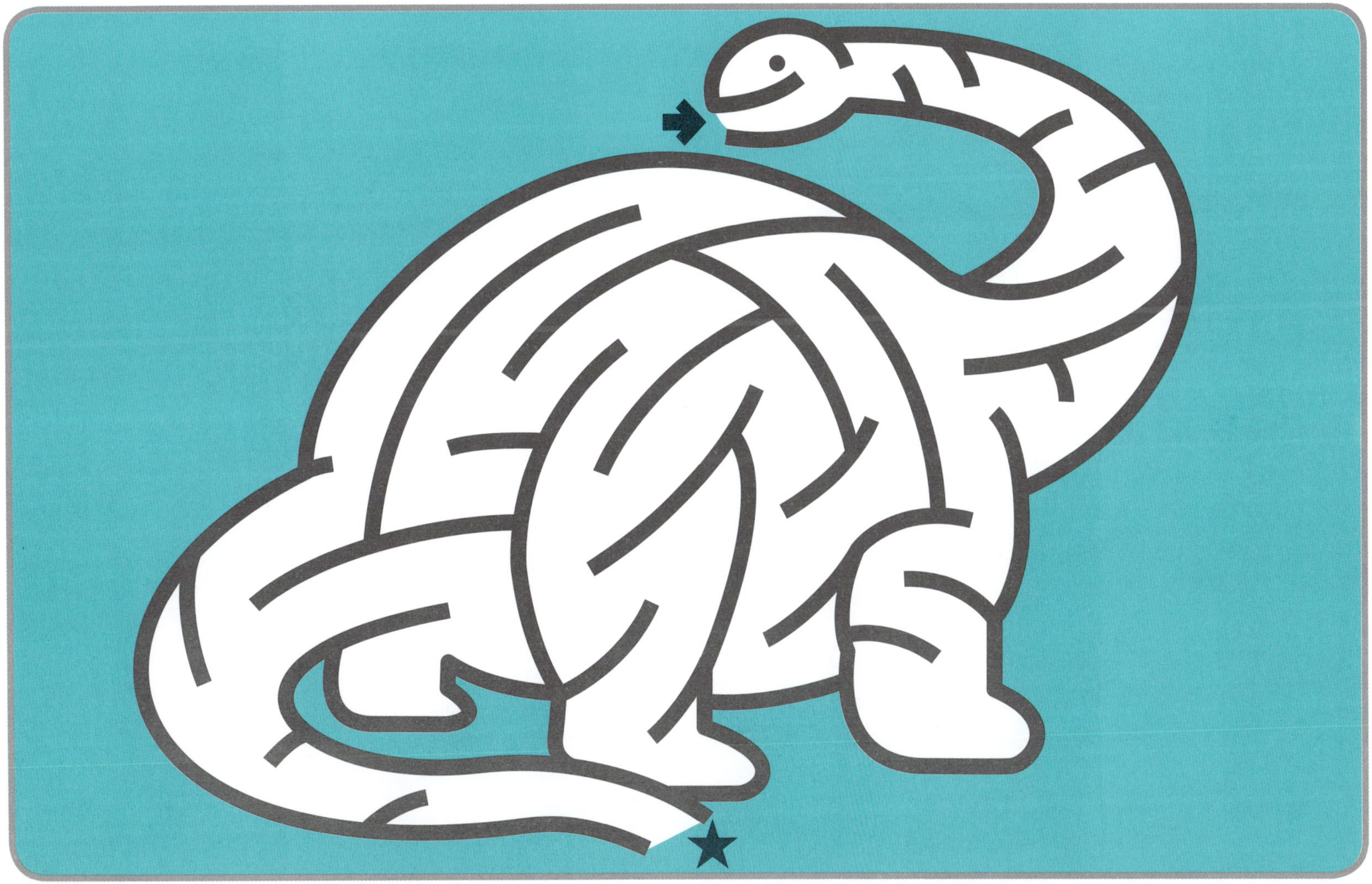

■ Draw a line from the arrow (➡) to the star (★) by following the path.